KEEPER OF THE FLAME

A BIOGRAPHY OF NINA SIMONE

JENNIFER WARNER

LifeCaps Biography Series
ANAHEIM, CALIFORNIA

Contents

About LifeCaps

LifeCaps is an imprint of BookCaps™ Study Guides. With each book, a lesser known or sometimes forgotten life is recapped.

We publish a wide array of topics (from baseball and music to literature and philosophy), so check our growing catalogue regularly (www.bookcaps.com) to see our newest books.

INTRODUCTION

The life of Nina Simone is one of blocked paths and surprising detours. Some people are born to an obvious destiny, only to find that society, circumstance, and chance steer them onto an entirely different course. Had Nina been born at a different time, she could very well have been a superstar of classical music at an early age. However, the severe oppression of African Americans in the United States during the 1950s forced her to find her fate down a different road. That she did so with flair, grace, and brilliance speaks to the resilience of the oppressed spirit.

Growing up poor in North Carolina, Nina was surrounded by the richness of music and spiritual faith. Her own musical talents materialized when she was a young child and they were fostered by her family. They could see that Nina was destined to become great and they did their best to allow her to shine. Nina performed at many church functions and local concerts, learning the important lesson of how to perform with an audience, rather than just for one. Educated in classical music, Nina prepared to begin a distinguished career as a virtuoso. However, that career had to wait. Her response to the sinister legacy of slavery, which threatened all of her dreams, was nothing short of genius.

Nina fought, as many great artists of her day did, to triumph against the forces arrayed against her. She blended her classical and gospel training with pop music to create a hybrid for which she would become famous. Working on stage through the tumultuous 1960s, she brought her music talents to bear for the Civil Rights Movement. A vocal opponent of the oppression of the African American community, Simone included songs of resistance in all of her performances during this time. Unlike Dr. Martin Luther King, she often advocated a more separatist approach. She decided that was the only way that African Americans would ever be treated as equals in the United States.

Simone was at the forefront of important, defining movements in the history of the United States. She was close friends with some of the greatest African American writers from this time in history: Langston Hughes, Lorraine Hansberry, and James Baldwin. They encouraged her art and pushed her to be a prominent voice in a community that was often forcibly silenced. She took their lesson well.

A strong, proud woman, Simone also spoke to the Women's Rights Movement. She combatted the stereotypes that often entrapped women, writing about the issues in her songs. For Simone, the central problem was a lack of pride. She urged women, especially African

American women, to embrace a fierce confidence and self-esteem. There are many female singers today who cite Nina Simone as profoundly influential to both their careers and their ability to navigate such obstacles with determination.

Whenever Nina played for an audience, she seemed commanding and powerful. She would often stand on stage before she began a concert, staring out at the thousands who had come to see her. She sang and played the piano like an enchantress, using her songs to capture her audience in a spell. Often using elements of heavy silence and hypnotic drum beats, many of Nina's performances seemed more like a ritual than entertainment. Those who witnessed her live performances said the experience was indescribable. Her approach to music later earned her the title, "The High Priestess of Soul."

Nina left the United States, only to become just as popular and influential abroad. Her ability to touch the hearts of audiences around the world speaks to her indomitable spirit and talent. Though she battled terrible oppression, the greed of managers and lovers, and her own mental illness, she refused to allow the trials of life to stand in her way. What she left behind is a testament to the power of the human spirit, beautifully recorded in song.

[1]
The Early Years

Nina grew up in the town of Tryon, North Carolina. In the early 1900s, before the Great Depression, Tryon was a typical poor community. Prohibition had transformed the town into a destination for wealthy white tourists who wanted to enjoy the local moonshine. It was one of the few ways that a poor family could earn an income in Tryon. Although the African American and white communities were technically separated, as they were in most of the country, Tryon was relatively peaceful. Violence between the white and African American communities was rare.

Both of Nina's parents were direct descendants of slavery. The exact history of John's family is somewhat mysterious, but Mary Kate's father was born a slave and died young. Nina's father, John, was universally liked by all those who met him. He had an aptitude for music and spent his early life singing and dancing for money. Nicknamed the "Whistler," John could whistle two tunes at the same time. He was far less conservative than his wife and counted many friends in the community. His children loved his easy-going nature and he was considered the more playful and affectionate parent.

John had aspirations to eventually succeed in business and earn his fortune, but his growing family demanded an immediate, steady income. When the Waymons moved to Tryon in 1929, they already had four children to support, with a fifth arriving not long after. The Waymons' third child, Harold, became partially paralyzed after a bout with meningitis. John took work both as a barber and as a dry cleaner to support his family. The Waymons were far from wealthy, but their daily needs were met. It was not long before John began to work toward his goal as a businessman.

John's wife, Mary Kate, came from a long line of devout Methodists. Her background led to her eventual ordination and she became a Methodist minister. The religious atmosphere of Tryon was rather unique in the country at that time. Although segregation was the law, the religious communities of the town did not strictly observe the practice. Whether it was Baptist, Pentecostal, or Methodist, the preachers of each religion worked together. In a small town, with lack of space, both white and African American communities shared churches. The Waymon children grew up with a strict, but fair, religious background and in a supportive community. Before tragedy hit the nation, their lives were comfortable. All of that changed in 1930 with the stock market crash and the beginning of the Depression.

The town of Tryon was as devastated as the rest of the country. The poor class suffered this misfortune the hardest. John's dreams of becoming wealthy due to his business disappeared and he lost his job. Without steady income, he was forced to take whatever temporary work he could find. Mary Kate also had to take on jobs outside of the church. Fortunately for the Waymons, food was less of an issue than for most. They had a small garden which they cultivated for their daily needs. The family began to transform their home into a mini-farm, complete with livestock. They often traded what excess they had for staples that they lacked.

Nina Simone was born on February 21st, 1933. Her birth name was Eunice Kathleen Waymon. As a child, she recalled the singing of her parents and the playing of the family organ at home. Her life was surrounded by music, despite the hard times that her family endured. Both of her parents were avid singers and the sounds of gospel music often filled the household. All of Nina's siblings were also involved in music, in one form or another. Nina began to sing at a very early age and she practiced playing on the family piano. The piano was so important to the Waymons that it was one of the first items saved when their house caught fire in 1935.

By the time she was three, Nina displayed an uncanny knack for music. She had perfect pitch. Nine would only have to hear a song played once before she could repeat it flawlessly. Her parents noticed her aptitude immediately and fostered it, sitting her down at the piano whenever there was time. Nina took to the lessons well, and could play more complicated pieces by the time she was four years old. Her mother had become an established member of the Tryon spiritual community and word quickly spread of little Nina's amazing ability with music. Most thought it was a divine gift. When she was just four years old, Nina played the organ for her mother's church services.

By the time Nina was six years old, she began to learn the more complicated hymns and songs of the spiritual community. Within her mother's church, Nina learned a sense of rhythm, style, and spontaneity. Although she had to memorize the music she might play for a specific service, that music often took a backseat to the organic process of preaching. The minister, or the congregation, might call for a variety of songs, depending on the spiritual mood at the time. An organist had to be prepared to play the requests. As Nina grew up, her musical life was dominated by the necessities of the church, but she often practiced and enjoyed other types of music. As a minister, though, Nina's mother demanded that her family be a model of spiritual purity and integrity. Mary Kate did not want any member of her household to bring shame on the family name. Consequently, Nina was not allowed to perform any music that was not spiritual while she was in public. She began to practice show tunes and popular music while in private, with the help of her father.

By 1938, Nina's father had become sick and her mother was often absent, due to her religious obligations. John could barely get out of bed and Nina tended to him. When Mary Kate was deeply immersed in her ministry, often traveling for days to preach, most of the work of raising the Waymon children fell to the oldest daughter, Lucille. Lucille took to her position with a natural grace. Nina eventually came to regard her as a mother figure and later wrote that her sister was both beautiful and tough. Lucille taught Nina that a woman could be strong, as well as attractive. Although these early years were hard for Nina and her family, who struggled to stay above water during the Depression, they instilled in her a lifelong love of music.

Nina's father eventually recovered from his illness and continued to pursue his various business interests. With the money he made, and Mary Kate's extra jobs outside of the church, the family survived and even prospered a bit. Mary Kate often cleaned houses to supplement the family income. One of Mary Kate's clients, the widow Katherine Miller, took an interest in Nina, having heard tales of her musical talent. She asked to see Nina play the piano.

Nina, with her two sisters Lucille and Dorothy, often performed for the community of Tryon. Taking the stage at the Tryon Theatre, the three singers called themselves the Waymon Sisters. When Mrs. Miller heard the young Nina on the piano, she was stunned at the skill and beauty of Nina's playing. She told Mary Kate that Nina needed special lessons so that her natural talent might be enhanced. When Mary Kate informed her that there was little money to pay for such lessons, Mrs. Miller offered to finance the lessons for one year. Mrs. Miller was already acquainted with a teacher by the name of Muriel Mazzanovich. When approached with the proposition, Mrs. Mazzanovich accepted. Nina's formal piano education began in 1939 with a woman she called, "Mrs. Mazzy."

Educating the Prodigy

For the next five years, Nina walked two miles to Mrs. Mazzy's house every Saturday. The walk became very habitual. First, Nina crossed the railroad tracks and walked down to a local pharmacy where she would purchase a grilled cheese sandwich. She had to eat the sandwich outside, standing up, because African Americans were not allowed to sit inside the pharmacy. She then proceeded to walk to the woods, where her lesson took place in a small house that was filled with pianos and art. The first time she met Mrs. Mazzy, Nina could barely breathe due to excitement. Mrs. Mazzy's house was small, but beautiful, and filled with her husband's artwork. Mrs. Mazzy was a tiny, refined English woman, who went about the business of teaching music in a very efficient way. Nina became entranced with her immediately.

Mrs. Mazzy put the little prodigy through the paces. After teaching Nina the basics of hand positions on the piano, Mrs. Mazzy moved on to more complicated lessons using a solfeggio method. This taught Nina how to mentally hear the pitches of music that she learned. Mrs. Mazzy also educated Nina on rhythms, melodies, harmonies, basic singing, and the proper body positioning needed to play the piano well. At first, Nina practiced three hours a day. By the time she reached the age of eleven, she practiced up to eight hours a day to perfect her craft.

Early on, Mrs. Mazzy introduced Nina to the music of a composer that would become a lifelong love: Johann Sebastian Bach. Bach's complicated musical pieces were very difficult for Nina at first. She despaired of ever mastering the highly technical math behind his compositions. With painstaking patience, and Mrs. Mazzy's steadfast encouragement, Nina worked through her fear and mastered the composer. In honor of Bach, Nina later incorporated his music into her own songs. She believed him to be her first serious step into professional music. Nina became familiar with other classical composers as well. They began to shape how she thought and practiced music, transforming her talent into what would become a classical powerhouse.

Mrs. Mazzy gave Nina a very thorough music education, one rarely given to an African American at that time in American history. After the first year, when Mrs. Miller could no longer fund the lessons, Mrs. Mazzy devised a way to keep her student. She asked the churches and community of Tryon to begin an educational fund for Nina: the Eunice Waymon Fund. Mrs. Mazzy saw the extraordinary talent within the young girl. She wanted Nina to pursue a musical education far into the future. The community responded with more funds than were needed for the lessons, so they were reserved for Nina's later educational needs. As a condition for the fundraising, and to teach Nina the art of fine public performance, Mrs. Mazzy required that Nina perform for the community on a semi-regular basis. Although Nina had performed for the public countless times, both with her sisters and alone for the church, these classical performances were different. Mrs. Mazzy taught her the poise and grace that accompanied such formal recitals. The community looked forward to each show. Nina, who was already well-known in Tryon, became the pride of the town. At the age of ten, Nina became a symbol for both the poor and the African American communities. If she could become a success, then there was hope that anyone could succeed, despite adversity.

Mary Kate was very proud of her daughter, as was Mrs. Mazzy. In later years, Nina would state that the pressure she often felt during her youth was enormous. As a child, she loved creating music. But when she became obligated to play for her community, she realized that it was for more than just entertainment. There were a great many hopes resting on her continued success. Both her family and her beloved piano teacher wanted her to become the first black concert pianist in the United States. Nina felt the pressure of those expectations on a daily basis. It was not long before she also realized that those pressures were intensely magnified because of racial boundaries. In one incident, when Nina was eleven, she found herself faced with the reality of the racial divide that would come to dominate much of her life. During that first encounter, there were hints of the civil rights activism that would later engage her.

Before the start of one of her frequent recitals, she looked down to find that her parents were no longer in the front row of the theatre. As Nina's popularity grew, more people attended her concerts. The Waymons had been forced to give up their seats to prominent members of the white community. Nina stood up from the piano and refused to play until her parents were returned to their proper place in the theatre. Although the Waymons were given their seats back, Nina could see that members of the audience laughed at her audacity. She realized that her position as the town star was far more precarious than she had known. Talent and hard work were not enough for an African American child or their family. In the end, they were still only second-class citizens.

Nina's lessons ended when she was twelve years old. In 1945, she left for a boarding school in Asheville. It was the first time she had been away from home. Although the school was staffed entirely by white teachers, the piano instructor was a personal friend of Mrs. Mazzy. Nina's tuition was paid out of the fund that Tryon had collected over the years. The boarding school was tough, with rigorous discipline, but Nina took to it very well. Her grades were some of the highest, and her piano lessons continued under new instruction. She graduated in 1950 at the top of her class. Her entire family traveled to witness her honors. True to her dedication to her student, Mrs. Mazzy arranged for Nina to prepare for further music education at the Curtis Institute in Philadelphia. To ready herself for the entrance exam, Nina would study for two months at the famous Juilliard School of Music in New York.

At the age of seventeen, Nina traveled to New York to stay with a friend of her mother's in the community of Harlem. By 1950, Harlem had already become a major hub of African American culture, including literature, theatre, and music. The Harlem Renaissance of the 1930s ensured that some of the greatest minds of the African American community migrated in and around Harlem. Although Nina was the only African American student at Juilliard while she was there, she was not the first African American musician to study at the school; Miles Davis had attended the same program. Nina studied harder than she had ever done in her life. She had very little money left to support her from the education fund gifted to her from her community scholarship. If she was not accepted at the Curtis Institute, her future was uncertain. In anticipation of that acceptance, her family moved to Philadelphia.

Before the exam came, Nina's family reported that she practiced seven to eight hours a day. She practiced until she nearly dropped from exhaustion. She worked from a list of the pieces she was required to play. They were to serve as examples of her mastery of the classics and the piano. She was already familiar with each of them. When the fated day arrived, Nina's father took her to her exam. After finishing the audition, Nina left. She never gave any details as to what exactly occurred during that time.

She and her family returned home to await word from the institute. It came just days later. In front of her entire family, who awaited the decision with tense excitement, Nina opened the letter that she had received. She had been denied entry into the program at Curtis. Nina was devastated. In her mind, she had failed herself, her family, her teachers, and the entire community that had worked so hard to support and nurture her.

The Prodigy Rejected

Nina never fully recovered from that terrible rejection. It haunted her until her death, many years later. Initially the family took it very hard as well, especially when the news of the rejection reached the town of Tryon. Many in her community had looked forward to watching

Nina's great talent blossom into a shining career. The rejection became all the more bitter when Nina's uncle, informed by his contacts, announced that Nina had been rejected simply because she was an African American woman. Nina could not accept that all of her dreams, for which she had fought and trained for so long, were over. She vowed that she would try the exam again the following year. The Waymon family tried to move on from the situation as quickly as they could. For them, racism and injustice was a fact of African American life. There seemed to be no reason to dwell on the inevitable.

Nina found a job assisting a local photographer, but she could not stay away from her beloved piano for long. Carrol, her brother, helped convince her to return to music. Nina used the rest of the money from her scholarship funds and employed the services of Vladimir Sokhaloff. Sokhaloff was a famous piano teacher who worked and played music at the Curtis Institute. With his instruction, Nina intended to return to Juilliard so that she could pursue her dream of becoming a concert pianist. Nina left the photographer and became a piano accompanist. She saved money and eventually moved into her own apartment in Philadelphia, in 1954.

Those first few months in Philadelphia were lonely and sad for Nina. She continued her lessons and her work as an accompanist. Eventually it made more sense to work independently, so she secured her own students. The work was hardly fulfilling, however, as Nina felt she had been reduced to a teacher, rather than a musician. Nina's love life was unfulfilling as well. The few relationships she had tried ended quickly. The pain and devastation of her professional life, completely derailed, was the only force that drove her to continue. She felt that she had to redeem herself as a musician. Sometime in late 1954, she finally got her chance. She met Faith Jackson.

Faith was a well-known prostitute in Philadelphia. Her charisma and strength were undeniable. Nina was drawn to her right away and the two became close friends. Nina hid the friendship from her family, especially her mother, whom she knew would never approve. Faith introduced Nina to the nightclub circuit and invited Nina to travel with her to Atlantic City, New Jersey. Nina discovered that she could make far more money playing in the bar scene of the famous gambling town than by offering piano lessons. It was a difficult choice for her, as she had never before been in a bar. Her family was not likely to approve of such a job. However, the lessons with Sokhaloff, and Nina's desire to return to music school, required that she save as much money as she could. Asking around, she secured a job with her first club in July.

That first night, she played only the piano. The bar owner, however, told her that she would have to sing if she intended to keep her job for long. Nina began to sing along with the music she played the very next evening. Although she had never really focused on singing before, she had the training to do so. She knew which songs would best complement her vocal range. To hide from her family the fact that she worked in such a place, she took the stage name "Nina Simone." "Nina" was a nickname from an old boyfriend, and meant "little one" in Spanish. "Simone" came from the first name of a French actress whom Nina admired, Simone Signoret. Although she played for a rowdy audience, under an assumed name, Nina's career as a musician had begun.

Nina developed her own style quickly, and with her audience in mind. The job required her to play seven hours a night and could quickly become repetitive. Nina began to improvise. She wove together classical pieces, modern pop, jazz, and the spiritual tunes of her youth into a music that was uniquely hers. It was not long before she established a following that came to the bar just to hear her play. They enjoyed the fiery young piano player's style. She did not tolerate a rude audience, and her mastery of music seemed to be effortless. By the time she returned home to Philadelphia at the end of the summer season, the small bar she played at became very successful.

[2]
THE ENTERTAINER EMERGES

Nina returned to Atlantic City the next year, in the summer of 1956, to play piano and sing for the same bar. It was there that she met Ted Axelrod. Ted shared a deep love and appreciation of music and he quickly became one of Nina's biggest fans. He came to the bar every night just to hear Nina play. Eventually he approached her and the two became friends. It was Axelrod who introduced Nina to a version of the song, "I Loves You, Porgy" from George Gershwin's opera. Nina fell in love with the tune, as sung by Billie Holiday, and began to sing a version of her own in just a few days. Gershwin's opera had been a huge success and many African American singers had performed versions of its music. Nina's rendition of "I Loves You, Porgy" was very popular with her audience.

Nina returned to Philadelphia after that season, but only to begin wrapping up her life as a teacher. She no longer wanted to work for substandard wages. She used her contacts to secure other nightclub jobs in Atlantic City, as well as Philadelphia, and finally informed her family about her new career. Her parents' opinions differed completely. Her mother was disappointed in the choice, believing that the music Nina played was ungodly. Her father supported her, however, as he himself had been an entertainer. That support came with a warning of the dangers such a life could bring. Nina left Philadelphia again and returned to play full-time in the bars of Atlantic City in 1956. It proved to be a very significant year, in both her career and her life.

After one of her performances, for which she was rapidly becoming famous both for her playing style and her temper, Nina met Don Ross. Ross was a drifter and he admired the rising star. It was not long before the two began a whirlwind romance that eventually became a short-lived marriage. Although Ross was quite charming, he seemed to have little ambition. He worked for the carnival circuit, but only for short periods, whenever he needed money. Nina's parents accepted him readily enough, even though he was a white man. The Waymons had never been prone to prejudice.

Nina also met the music agent, Jerry Fields, that year. He sought her out when her fame in the Atlantic City bars began to spread. Fields promised to make a record with Nina in New York and convinced her to follow him to the town of New Hope. He wanted her to get a wider audience. While in New Hope, Nina befriended the guitarist, Alan Schackman. Schackman had gained fame working for such musicians as Burt Bacharach. Nina found a great rapport with Schackman and the two musicians became lifelong friends. She worked with Schackman to produce a demo tape, which included a version of the song, "I Loves You, Porgy," first introduced to her by Axelrod.

Nina's agent sent her to meet with record producer, Syd Nathan, who owned King Records. Syd Nathan later became famous for being notoriously hard to work with, and for accusations that he cheated his musicians out of their profits. This was not a rare occurrence in the music industry, especially for African American musicians. Unfortunately, Nina was new to the scene and prospects were scarce. If she wanted to break into the music industry, she would have to take a chance. She refused to work with the songs that Nathan wanted recorded, however, and demanded that she be allowed to pick the music. He agreed and she recorded her first album with King Records: Little Girl Blue.

That album became her first, but it was not completely original material. Most of the music covered earlier songs that had become hits. It did allow Nina to display her great skill with the piano, with two instrumental pieces she wrote during the session. The entire album was recorded in a single thirteen hour session and would later cause much controversy. True to many music contracts at that time, Nina was given a single sum for her work. She was paid $3,000 and signed away any rights to royalties from future sales of the album. It would become a tragic mistake many years later, although one that was all-too-common in the music industry at the time. If musicians wanted to make any money at all from their music, they had to take such deals. Often, they had no real understanding of the consequences until it became too late.

The money she made from the album allowed Nina to continue her lessons with Sokhaloff. She had never abandoned her dream of reentering the Juilliard School of Music so that she might become a great, classical pianist. For her, playing the club scene continued to be nothing more than a means to an end. With the news that she had a soon-to-be-released album, her agent secured her jobs in several clubs in New York City. She traveled back and forth between New York and Philadelphia, spending time with Don Ross, continuing her lessons with Sokhaloff, and playing in various locations. Her style was now well-known in the local music scene: brilliant piano pieces delivered with smooth, smoky vocals, as well as a good dose of anger should the crowd become too unruly. She was billed as a jazz artist, which was a description she disliked. She would prefer to be known as a classical musician, rather than a player of popular tunes.

In 1958, her first album was finally released. Nina wanted to promote the album and she tried to contact Syd Nathan. He refused to speak with her. Nina was confused by his behavior and it seemed that she was on her own. The album received some good reviews, but without a wider audience there was very little chance that it would gain traction with the public. The entire album almost passed into the annals of history with little note. Fortunately for Nina, the audience she needed came from a popular DJ from Philadelphia.

Nina had met Sid Marx a few times while playing in Philadelphia. He approached her numerous times, always encouraging her to continue. In the 1950s, DJs had enormous power in the music industry. They were responsible for crafting their own shows, and their likes and dislikes could literally launch or destroy a music career. Sid Marx fell in love with Little Girl Blue. He especially liked, "I Loves You, Porgy" and played it daily, sometimes several times in a row. It was not long before the public began to ask for the song, forcing other DJs to play it. Nina's rendition of the Gershwin tune could be heard on radios in a large portion of the United States. The pressure of the song's popularity forced Syd Nathan to release the song as a single. By 1959, Nina Simone hit the R&B music charts and she was on her way to becoming a household name.

Nina's agent convinced her to move to New York permanently. Fields wanted her to capitalize on her success without the hassle of having to travel back and forth between cities. She returned home to deliver the news to her boyfriend, Don, and the two married in a quick, private ceremony. She arrived in New York, Don in tow, and the two settled in a small apartment in Greenwich Village. Their relationship was doomed from the start. Don refused to find steady work. Instead, he lived off the money that Nina brought in from her performances at the nightclubs. He drank heavily and spent most of his time entertaining friends. Eventually Nina had to secure a side-job as a maid just to make ends meet. Success was far from what she had envisioned.

Nina's life was harrowing for those months in 1959. She worked up to fourteen hours a day, playing music and cleaning, and it eventually took its toll on her. She began to drink and often hid her money from Don, so that she could afford her trips to Philadelphia to continue her piano lessons. Don was of no help to her and she could no longer afford the damage to her body and mind that supporting them both brought. In less than two months, the couple split up and Nina walked out on her husband. She found a small apartment for herself and tried to get her life back in order. She quit drinking heavily and focused on her career.

Nina's agent was very good at finding her jobs, but what she needed was a manager. She contacted Fields about the matter and he introduced her to the lawyer, Max Cohen. Cohen appreciated Nina's classical background and began to manage her financial affairs. He was very good at his job and became one of the first real friends that Nina made in the city. She also met Joyce Selznick, who was a talent scout for Colpix Records. Selznick had followed Nina's musical success with enthusiasm and wanted her to sign a multi-record deal. Nina did so, with Cohen's help, and began to record the first album in 1959.

The first Colpix record, The Amazing Nina Simone, was released very quickly. It won her critical success and allowed her to display her skill with the piano. It also showed her how the music industry worked. Not long before the album hit the record stores, another one entitled Nina Simone and Her Friends was released by King Records. It included songs that were discarded from Nina's first album with Syd Nathan. It was meant to capitalize on her success, competing with her contract at Colpix. Syd Nathan had never contacted her about the album, nor was he required to do so. He owned those songs and could distribute them however he liked. Nina's lawyer, Cohen, explained the contract she had signed to her in detail. It shattered her view of the recording industry. She began to despise the whole affair, seeing nothing but crooks and criminals who preyed on the talents of others. Her beliefs were backed by hard evidence, as the rise of the pirated record industry included tracks of her music that had been stolen from some of her live performances.

Although she had not been paid for all of her work, Nina's albums, released by both Colpix and King Records, had established her as a major musical talent. She played to sold-out crowds in clubs all across New York City, and she played as she wished. She no longer bowed to the pressures of owners, or the fickle desires of her audience. Her repertoire included whatever she selected, and it was non-negotiable. She also demanded to receive a portion of whatever the clubs charged at the door for her performances. She felt that it was her name and reputation that brought the crowds. Nina was no longer happy with receiving only a flat fee for her performances. Her reputation as fiery-tempered also grew. She could lash out at a crowd whenever she felt they were disrespectful, coming and going as they pleased, or if their chatter became too loud. She brought this attitude with her in her negotiations with promoters and managers, as well. Nina was now a star and she acted like one. If that included an element of being a diva, she felt she had certainly earned it.

Nina's agent arranged for a special performance to capitalize on her rising fame. He wanted to elevate her from the venue of bars and clubs and put her in a more formal setting. He secured the Town Hall, a famous theatre in New York known for fine, classical performances. For the first time, Nina had a show that catered to her fondest dreams of becoming a classical pianist. Cohen spared no expense and invited all of the New York elite, as well as journalists and influential music producers. Nina prepared herself for a magnificent show, one that would secure her reputation for the future.

On September 12th, 1959, Nina performed in the Town Hall, in front of an expectant audience. Her show was recorded by Colpix records and later released as an album. Nina's music selections moved through classical pieces, traditional ballads, and show tunes, including songs from the Gershwin opera that she had tailored to suit her own, unique style. She also played familiar pieces from the singer, Billie Holiday. The performance was a resounding success. The audience fell in love with Nina's skill and poise. The next day she relished the rave reviews for her music in all of the major city newspapers. She no longer had to worry about establishing a musical career.

It was an exciting time to live in New York. Greenwich Village was the home and gathering place of some of the greatest intellectuals and artists of the era. Nina soon came to know and befriend many of them. She developed relationships with great writers, such as Langston Hughes, Amiri Baraka, and James Baldwin. Hughes and Baldwin, in particular, had a profound effect on her. They introduced Nina to literary culture, as well as a long fight that consumed the African American community: the Civil Rights Movement. Nina also began to perform at the Village Vanguard, a legendary playhouse that hosted such great musical talents as Miles Davis and Dizzy Gillespie, with opening acts from comedians like Bill Cosby and Richard Pryor. Greenwich Village was also a home base for great folksingers and songwriters as well, including Joan Baez and Bob Dylan.

Although she played at the Vanguard often, Nina also toured. She could be found in Washington, Chicago, and Philadelphia. The money from her success poured in and she moved into a lavish apartment in the Village. She also bought a luxury car and spent many of her free hours just enjoying the freedom it brought her, as she toured around the city. She continued her lessons with Sokhaloff and often sent money home to her family. She had finally found the success and acclaim she sought, but her family rarely shared it with her. Her parents, especially, made almost no note of her rising fame. It was a sore point for Nina, and one that made her feel lonely despite the crowds that roared her name.

Nina finally divorced Don Ross in 1960, though he often attended her performances after that. The two had a falling out that would never be healed, but Nina invited him to attend her shows to combat her loneliness. She now had a place to call home, but she was rarely there. She toured relentlessly across the country and the pace took a toll on her energy. Nina worried that her success was limited and that it could lose steam at any time. She later explained that it was fear of losing her momentum that drove her to such a grueling schedule.

She was invited to perform at the Newport Jazz Festival in 1960, and she accepted. Her record company, Colpix, recorded the show and released the performance as her second live album. By this time, Alan Schackman had become a great friend and he almost always accompanied her on the stage as her guitarist. It was one of the first times that Nina moved from her usual set tunes and allowed her African roots to flavor her music. She enchanted the audience with a song entitled, "Flo Me La." It was an African chant often used during ritualized walks. The audience took a few minutes to warm up to the tune, but with the mesmerizing drumbeat and Nina's silky voice, it was a hit. Nina's inclusion of such a song hinted at the activism that would soon engage her life. Nina was no longer content to play music she felt catered to the white masses, or that boxed her into easily defined musical categories. She began to break free of such confines, establishing herself as an African American artist.

Although the Supreme Court of the United States ended segregation in 1954, that decision began a long battle between African Americans and white separatists. Segregation was officially declared illegal, but it was still practiced in many parts of the United States. Unfortunately, the unofficial fight around segregation led to a great deal of violence against the African American community. The white population who was unwilling to accept racial integration spawned an era of horror and reprisal, which would culminate in the Civil Rights Movement of the 1960s.

[3]
THE WIFE AND MOTHER

Nina met Andrew Stroud after a performance one night in late 1960. With her touring schedule still frantic, she played at the Basin Street East nightclub in New York. As she surveyed the audience, she saw her hairdresser sitting with an unknown man. He was light-skinned, wore an African medallion, and was very attractive. During a break in the show, she moved down to sit at the table and chatted with them all. After their introduction, Stroud claimed to be a bank teller and later invited Nina on a date. She accepted and the two left the

Village after her show to spend time together in Harlem.

Over the course of two dates, it quickly became apparent to Nina that Stroud was a well-known figure in Harlem. Many people knew him by name, and often deferred to him out of respect and fear. He seemed to cast a charm wherever he went, with his quiet intensity and calm demeanor. Nina was caught in his spell almost immediately. At the end of their second date, he finally told her that he was not a bank teller. He was a police officer. Harlem was his precinct and that explained why everyone knew him very well.

During their short courtship, Nina began to hear many dark rumors about her suitor. He was not a man that anyone wanted to anger and he always got his way. Nina received a hint of his true personality after one of their dates. When she denied him entry into her apartment, he told her that he got what he wanted. Using a skeleton key, he opened the locked door to make a point. Waving goodbye, he left her alone that night.

Nina soon found him to be a constant presence. She would find flowers and gifts backstage after her performances, including expensive jewelry. She wondered how he could afford such items on his salary, but she ignored her intuition. He made her feel safe and eased her loneliness, despite her reservations about his reputation. The two officially became a couple and she introduced him to her friends. It was apparent to all that Nina and Andrew would soon wed, despite any reservations that she might have had.

Nina could hardly worry about the direction that her relationship would soon take. In early 1961, she was invited to play at the Apollo Theatre in Harlem. The Apollo was the home base for some of the greatest African American musical talent in America. To be invited to play there was a great honor, one that she could not decline. To play at the Apollo was no easy feat, however, even for a seasoned performer. Although the theatre had hosted the performances of many African American musicians, including James Brown and Billie Holiday, it was a notorious venue. The audiences could be cruel and very critical. If they disliked a performer, they were not afraid to show it. To survive a performance there, a performer had to have thick skin and razor sharp wits. Nina was ready.

Although she was terribly nervous, she played as well as she ever had. When she tried to introduce one of her songs, some members of the crowd laughed at her. She stopped, addressed the audience, and lectured them on the manners needed to attend such a performance. The audience seemed to listen and she continued. As she played, she saw three women approach the stage. They pulled coins out of their purses and scattered them at her feet. It was a gesture of contempt and it was not lost on Nina. The rest of the performance continued without a hitch, but she vowed to never play at the Apollo again. She was invited to return several times over the next few years, but she never accepted.

In the summer of 1961, Nina began to feel ill. She ignored her symptoms, though, and traveled to a show in Philadelphia. Backstage, she collapsed and later awoke in a hospital. Her boyfriend, Andrew Stroud, was by her side. The doctors told Nina that they were unsure whether she had a mild form of polio, or spinal meningitis. The prospect of meningitis terrified her. It was the same disease that had wreaked such damage on her brother, Harold. It was never discovered what exactly Nina suffered with and she left the hospital after a few weeks. Andrew pushed for Nina to marry him, and the couple became officially engaged. Her family and friends celebrated. Nina's mother was charmed by Stroud, but her father eyed him warily.

During an engagement party in August, Stroud's violent side finally revealed itself. He was very quiet the entire evening and Nina noticed that he drank heavily. Later, one of Nina's fans rushed to her for an autograph and then handed her a note, which she automatically put into her pocket. It was an event of no importance to her, as it had happened many times. Stroud believed that the note implied something else, however, and began to shout at Nina. When he stormed out of the party, she chased him out to the street. He punched Nina in the face and forced her into a cab. The beating continued throughout the ride to her apartment, as well as in the street, the building itself, and into the apartment. Stroud tied her to a chair, held a gun to her head, and demanded that she explain herself. He beat her for hours. When she was finally so exhausted that she could barely speak, Stroud dragged Nina into her bedroom and sexually assaulted her. After he passed out, she fled the apartment to find safety with a friend.

Nina hid from Andrew for two weeks, until he finally found her in a coffee bar. He asked her where she had received the beating that was still evident on her face. In shock, she told him that he was the one who had assaulted her. Stroud seemed very confused and completely denied that he had done anything of the sort. Nina could not believe that he could forget the incident, but his sincerity finally convinced her. She demanded that he see a psychiatrist. Stroud made an appointment with two different doctors, and they reported their findings to Nina. The first told her that Stroud was very capable of violence and that she should not marry him. The second believed that Stroud had suffered from a bout of temporary insanity, brought on by the alcohol. He believed that Stroud would probably not repeat the incident.

Stroud seemed to have changed completely since the beating and showed no further signs of the savage violence he had displayed. Despite her misgivings, Nina decided that she would rather be married to a man that could protect her instead of living life alone. She married Stroud in December of 1961. The ceremony took place in her apartment. Though many of her friends from the music industry attended the wedding, her father did not. In just a few short days, she was again back on the road and traveled to the capital city, Lagos, in Nigeria.

She had been invited to attend a conference in the African nation by her friends, Langston Hughes and James Baldwin. Both men were great writers who worked toward establishing a strong, African American literary voice in the United States. They felt that Africa was the place to understand both their roots, and the course that Africans must set for their lives.

Many countries were fighting for their independence from colonial rule in Africa, since the country of Ghana had achieved it in 1957. For Hughes and Baldwin, there were hints to be found in these struggles of what needed to occur in the United States. It was a profound trip for Nina and began to shape who she would become later as an activist, fighting white oppression wherever she found it back home. Although she was surrounded by some of the most profound activists of the day, she had not really become a part of that activism.

Nina left Africa after just a few short days. She returned to New York and traveled to the new house in the suburb of Mount Vernon that her husband had purchased for the family. Stroud had three children, from former marriages, and he intended to start a family with Nina as well. His children visited often, but Nina was now wealthy enough to afford both a maid and a nanny. She was happy with the move, feeling that elements of a domestic life were what she needed to ground her after so many months spent on stage. Her home was always open to her friends, and she had frequent visitors. She also realized that her dream of becoming a concert pianist, in the formal way she had always envisioned, was essentially gone. She was a popular musician. Although it was not quite what she had wanted, it brought her a life of comfort and success. She accepted it.

As she continued to perform in New York, Philadelphia, and Chicago, Nina watched the unfolding drama of the African American struggle in the United States. By this time, Dr. Martin Luther King was a well-known figure in the fight against segregation. Civil unrest had already begun to simmer in the African American communities. The Montgomery bus boycotts had occurred, initiated by the bravery of Rosa Parks, and several black churches had been bombed in Alabama. The fight for equality was well underway. King was a hero to the African American community and many followed the course of his life very carefully.

Nina and Stroud settled into the more rural setting and began to plan the future of Nina's career. Stroud left his position as a police officer and became Nina's manager. She believed that he was the best person for the job. He had managerial experience and knew how to work with officials. Stroud quickly became very efficient at managing Nina's career. He handled all of Nina's bookings, as well as every dime of her finances. Nina allowed him complete access to her career and he made all of the decisions concerning it. Whenever there were legal contracts, Nina's lawyer, Cohen, would negotiate with Stroud over the particulars of each one. Nina continued to play her music and, in early 1962, she became pregnant. She still had her multi-album deal with Colpix to complete, however, and she worked until very late in her pregnancy. She released the Duke Ellington tribute album: Nina Sings Ellington.

Lisa Celeste was born in September of 1962. She took her middle name from a previous daughter of Stroud's who had died as a child. Nina loved being a mother and showered her daughter with affection. Stroud enjoyed being a father again, but he showed signs of jealousy whenever Nina spent too much time with her daughter. For the first time since Nina had begun her musical career, she finally took some time off to rest. She left for a long cruise in 1963. The time afforded to her by her prolonged rest began opening her eyes to many things.

Nina had been so busy with her career that she really had not become engaged in the events going on in the world around her. Although she had James Baldwin and Langston Hughes in her life, their conversations had been more of a distraction from Nina's busy musical life rather than a call to action. Now that she had time to reflect, she began to see that the struggle for equality going on in the African American community included her. It also included her daughter, whom Nina realized would have to grow up in a country that was divided. It was not a pleasant prospect. It took a special friend, however, to really motivate Nina to join the fight and take her place in the Black Movement.

[4]
THE ACTIVIST

Nina had become a famous singer and was already familiar with many of the great personalities who occupied the communities of Greenwich Village and Harlem, in New York. One of those individuals, Lorraine Hansberry, also counted Nina as a personal friend. Hansberry had made a name for herself as an important playwright. She was the first black, female playwright to have her creation produced on Broadway. Entitled A Raisin in the Sun, the play took its name from a famous line from one of Langston Hughes' poems. Hansberry was quite outspoken in her Pan-Africanist beliefs. Hughes and Baldwin were also Pan-Africanists, believing that the entire African race was connected, in both their sorrows and their triumphs. Nina finally began to connect the dots in her life, realizing that she was at the intellectual epicenter in a war against racism.

Hansberry, who had become Lisa Celeste's godmother, lived not far from Nina. The two women spent long afternoons discussing the Black Movement and the fight for liberation. Nina was exposed to the writings of Marx and the ideas that fueled liberation movements, both violent and nonviolent. She began to see Dr. Martin Luther King's struggle as a reflection of her own struggle. Hansberry began to convince her that it was impossible to be African American in the United States and not be a part of the Civil Rights Movement, especially if one were famous and had the power to command audiences. It was a compelling argument and it stayed with Nina.

Nina returned to the stage in an amazing performance at Carnegie Hall in April of 1963. It was later released as an album by her record label, Colpix, entitled: Nina Simone at Carnegie

Hall. That year would serve to change Nina's career path. Instead of making music just to entertain, she would craft music to serve a revolution. When Dr. Martin Luther King, along with other pastors, was arrested the same month as Nina's Carnegie performance, she received a phone call from Hansberry. Quite frankly, Hansberry asked what Nina was doing while the leaders of the liberation movement sat in jail. During Nina's later performance in Chicago, she considered including songs intended to inform the public about the struggle of the Black Movement. She had mentioned that struggle to her audiences, during some of her performances, but had never really organized her concerts around the cause. That changed at the end of 1963.

After President John F. Kennedy's announcement that he intended to introduce a Civil Rights Bill to Congress, acts of violence against the African American community increased. One of the most blatant displays was the death of Medgar Evers, a secretary for the NAACP, who was shot to death outside of his home in June. Then, in September, a bomb was hurled into a church in Birmingham, Alabama. Four African American girls were killed. The riots that ensued resulted in the death of more innocents. When Nina heard the news of the chaos erupting in Alabama, she became enraged. Not knowing what to do, she raced to her garage and began to collect various pieces of equipment. When her husband found her later in the house, he realized that she was trying to fashion a homemade gun. She wanted to lash out in any way that she could. Stroud convinced her that her actions would not solve the problem. After she finally calmed down, Nina realized that the best way she could help the Black Movement was to sing.

Nina felt a storm building within her that she could not contain. She immediately sat down at her piano and began to write a musical piece. In only an hour she created her first protest song, "Mississippi Goddam." It would become a battle cry for action and a song that she would sing many times over the years. Nina was less interested in non-violent protest than she was with change. If that change included violence, then so be it. "Mississippi Goddam" contained all of the rage and anger she felt at the injustices she saw in her world. She sang the song publicly for the first time in New York, at the Village Gate Theatre. It was an immediate hit with the audience. Nina's protest song resonated with her audience to a degree that she had never seen before. It was not long before Colpix released the song as a single, and it sold very well.

Nina had reached a crossroads in her career, one that she felt keenly. Up until her decision to become a part of the Black Movement, she felt that her life was essentially on autopilot. She had become famous and wealthy, but her music did not seem to have any higher purpose. She now realized that music could be a powerful agent for change. It gave her a way to contribute to a cause that directly influenced her life. She began to play at benefit concerts, gearing her music toward informing the public about the racial struggle that surrounded them.

Many African American musicians joined the fight at this time, and all of them worked under threat. When Nina played a concert at Miles College in Birmingham, Alabama, the mood was very tense. White extremists had threatened violence, and none of the performers had any reason to disbelieve them. Any protest concert could hold such menace, but this was especially true in the southern United States. Although she was frightened, Nina felt energized by the fact that her work was so important. If those who fought against desegregation felt the need to threaten such a concert, then obviously such concerts were working. They were having an impact on a public that desperately needed to hear the messages that such music brought.

When President Kennedy was assassinated in November of 1963, the country was in the midst of a deep divide between the African American and white populations. Violent riots had taken place in Illinois and Pennsylvania, as the Black Movement gained power. Dr. Martin Luther King's influential organization, the Southern Christian Leadership Conference (SCLC), had staged sit-ins and protests throughout the country. King represented the power of non-violent resistance, but there were others who felt that freedom from discrimination must come at any cost. Malcolm X, a powerful and influential leader of the Black Muslims in the United States, gave inflammatory speeches that spoke toward defiant resistance. He believed that the integration of the races in the United States was doomed to failure. Those in power, the white population, would always find a way to reassert their power. Only a separate state would give African Americans their autonomy and freedom. Other groups, such as the Student Nonviolent Coordinating Committee (SNCC), were a bit more toward the middle. Nina leaned much more toward this view. She believed that those in power would always try to keep that power. Non-violent protests were preferred, but if violence became necessary to defend the rights of the oppressed, then so be it.

Other events in the world seemed to mirror the struggle that took place in the United States, such as the arrest of the great African leader, Nelson Mandela, in South Africa. The struggles of the African American community in the United States culminated in the signing of the Civil Rights Act in the summer of 1964 by

President Johnson. Segregation became illegal. Nina now believed that change was not only possible, but imminent. It was a great victory, but the racial wounds of the country were far from healed.

In 1964, Nina changed her record label and signed a new contract with Philips Records. The head of Philips Records, Willem Langenberg, approached Nina backstage one night during a concert. He had fallen in love with Nina's music, and especially the song, "Mississippi Goddam." His company was the first to pursue Nina out of a genuine desire for her artistry, rather than just a chance to make money. Nicknamed "Big Willy," due to his enormous size, he charmed both Nina and her husband with dreams of taking her music to an international audience. Philips Records, based out of the Netherlands, had a broad reach and both Nina and Andrew knew that this was an opportunity that they could not pass up. Nina was no longer satisfied with Colpix records, who would eventually release the last two records of her multi-album contract without notifying her.

Nina produced two albums for Philips Records in a short amount of time. Big Willy had rapidly become one of Nina's closest friends and he believed that she played her best music live, without the benefit of a studio. He recorded two of those live concerts and converted the music into one album: Nina Simone in Concert. Nina's voice on the album is backed by a jazz quartet, and on it she placed some of her most personal pieces. They declared her African American heritage and rang with Nina's dedication to the fight for self-confidence and pride. Songs like "Old Jim Crow" and "Mississippi Goddam" are direct results of the African American fight against segregation and racism. Other songs on the album, like "Pirate Jenny," from the play, The Threepenny Opera, had a direct influence on other protest singers of the day. The album was an enormous success and displayed the width and breadth of Nina's talent. It introduced a larger audience to her music, allowing those who were not privy to a live concert to hear the magic that Nina could weave during her performances.

Nina's personality and performances in the mid-1960s began to show elements of the illness that she would hide for the duration of her life. She could fly into rages at the smallest provocation and many among the crew, on and off the stage, learned not to provoke her. It became understood that Nina's moods could fluctuate between high and low without any real reason behind the shifts. Most thought that she simply played the role of diva, certainly not unknown behavior for famous musicians. The fact that her psychological state could plummet just as fast, though, hinted at a darker reason for her actions. It would become a great problem for her in the future, but while she worked for Philips Records, she kept the issue a secret from the wider public.

The beginning of 1965 was a very sad time for Nina. Her long-time friend and confidant, Lorraine Hansberry, who had suffered from pancreatic cancer, died in January. Both Dr. Martin Luther King and James Baldwin sent condolences to the funeral, and Nina played a special song for her friend, "In the Evening by the Moonlight." Years later, in 1970, Nina would write a song dedicated to Hansberry. "To Be Young, Gifted, and Black" would become one of Nina's greatest hits. It was adopted as an anthem of the Civil Rights Movement, and was covered and recorded by numerous other musicians.

Nina played a concert again at Carnegie Hall, and this time, much of her family was in attendance. To her delight, her childhood piano teacher also sat in the audience. Later that year, Nina recorded the album, I Put a Spell on You, which reached number 23 on the United States R&B billboard charts. The title song was first written and performed by Screamin' Jay Hawkins in 1956, but before Nina covered it, the song had not achieved any major success. Nina's version was later covered by many other artists, and has also appeared in samples in various rap songs. She sang it in the smooth and bewitching way that had become a trademark for her. Nina's album became a great success in Europe as well, and began to establish Nina's reputation abroad. The album brought her further commercial success, but Nina continued to play at various benefits across the country.

In March of 1965, Nina left New York to appear at a concert in Montgomery. Dr. Martin Luther King organized a large march, beginning in Selma and ending in Montgomery, to protest for voting rights for the African American community. Although segregation had officially been declared illegal, it was still in common practice throughout much of the country, especially the south. African American voters were often violently denied the right to cast their ballots in any number of elections. King's march was a show of solidarity in the African American community.

Malcolm X was assassinated in February, and although he had been slain by members of his own organization, it reaffirmed that the fight for civil rights was both bloody and brutal. It was more important than ever to continue the momentum toward complete liberation and freedom. Nina and her players tried to fly into Montgomery for the concert, only to find that the runway had been blocked by bulldozers and trucks. Those who desired the continuation of segregation and separation knew about the planned concert and wanted it stopped.

The performers landed in the town of Jackson, Mississippi instead, and took a much smaller plane that allowed them to land outside of Montgomery. The stage, at the end of a soccer field, was surrounded by a large crowd awaiting the performers. Nina performed songs of protest, along with Harry Belafonte and Leonard Bernstein. She was accompanied by her long-time friend and guitarist, Alan Schackman. The efforts of King's protest, aided by such concerts, eventually led to the Voting Rights Act, which was signed by President Johnson in August of 1965. Not only was segregation illegal, now the country had to extend the right to vote to all adults, regardless of race.

Nina traveled to Europe that same year and gave her first concerts abroad. She played in London, as well as in Antibes, France. In Antibes, she played with Duke Ellington, a famous bandleader of jazz music. She had covered many of his songs in an album she released in 1962 — Nina Simone Sings Ellington — and she admired him very much. Although she returned to the United States after only a short time, she solidified her reputation as a musical talent in Europe.

Nina continued to record albums for Philips Records, and always included songs of protest and solidarity with the Black Movement. "Strange Fruit" was a notable example. First recorded by Billie Holiday in 1939, an artist Nina was often compared with, "Strange Fruit" was a direct commentary on the vile act of lynching. Right from the beginning of the days of slavery, lynching had always been a threat for the African American community. It was a horrible ritual by which an African American man or woman would be subjected to torture, and eventual hanging, at the hands of deranged white racists. The act was usually talked about in hushed tones, or silenced altogether. Bringing up the topic brought about understandable feelings of hostility and discord in both the African American and white communities. Billie Holiday's song brought the act out into the light and forced the public to look at it. Nina's rerecording of the song was understood in a larger context of the often violent end of racism. It was a bold move to release such a song, in the face of the upheaval that had torn the United States apart.

Among many of Nina's friends in the fight for civil rights were Stokely Carmichael and Miriam Makeba. Carmichael was the chairman of the SNCC. He later became a prominent member of the Black Panthers, a controversial organization aimed at taking a firm stand against all forms of oppression against the African American community. Miriam Makeba was a South African singer and activist who became highly influential in the Pan-African movement. The two would eventually marry for a time.

Both Carmichael and Makeba encouraged Nina to continue with her protest efforts as the fight continued to escalate. The country was in chaos with the struggle for Civil Rights and new riots threatened to spring up overnight. Whenever the African American community seemed to claim victory in one arena, a new round of violence or oppression began somewhere else. Nina despaired that there would never be any sort of equality between the two races. It bolstered her belief that a radical separation was the only course of action the African American community could take.

Nina's fight for the Civil Rights Movement in her music led her to write a new song in 1966. Although the fight for equality in the African American community was universal, Nina felt that the struggle was particularly difficult for women. The 1960s saw the rise of many movements, including the Women's Liberation Movement. Nina was at the forefront of this particular social change, which would not become formally organized until the late 1960s. She released an album entitled Wild Is the Wind that included the song, "Four Women." In it she tackled the stereotypes and roles that she felt African American women were often forced to play. The characters in the song moved through the racial spectrum, including dark and light-skinned women. "Four Women" met with mixed success, as many critics felt that it was inherently racist. Nina was angered that some listeners did not seem to understand the perspectives that she wished to illustrate. The song was banned from play in many radio stations, but Nina brought it to the live stage whenever she could.

The volume of concerts that Nina played began to take a toll on her toward the end of 1966. Her husband scheduled a grueling number of venues, often back to back, and Nina could never seem to catch her breath. She had also signed a new recording contract, with RCA, and was saddened to leave her friend Big Willy behind. Stroud had orchestrated the deal, as Nina's manager, and she felt a great deal of pressure with the new 10-album contract. She had little time to complain, however, as she was scheduled to tour the country with the popular African American comedian, Bill Cosby. Nina barely remembered many of the concerts she played. She seemed to walk around in a dream state and often had visions and hallucinations that she could not explain. Many times she arrived on stage late, and her famous rants toward the audience continued. Instead of criticizing her audience for their rude behavior, Nina now frequently lectured audiences on the need to educate themselves and become a part of the Civil Rights Movement. Nina finally finished the tour in early 1967.

Nina's friend, the writer Langston Hughes, died in September of 1967. In honor of him, she sang a tune that he had written called "Backlash Blues." It was released on her first record with RCA, Nina Simone Sings the Blues, and she intended it as a protest song. The lyrics spoke not only to the plight of African Americans in the United States, but also to the growing anti-war sentiment around the Vietnam conflict. Many of the civil rights battles now partnered their efforts in protests against the war. In a sad and ironic twist, it was an issue that could often unite whites and African Americans. Soldiers of both races were drafted to fight.

Later that year, Nina's previous record label, Philips, released an album of songs and live recordings of previously unpublished material. The High Priestess of Soul, the record's name, became the moniker that would follow Nina around for the rest of her life. She did not really enjoy the title, as she felt it too narrowly defined her musical focus. It was a title that she would carry for the rest of her career, however. Many felt that it accurately described the atmosphere of magic and ceremony that seemed to be a part of Nina's concerts.

When Dr. Martin Luther King died in 1968, the Civil Rights Movement, as it had been defined, began to unravel. Nina was in the midst of preparing for a concert when she learned that the great leader had been shot and killed by a white man. She despaired that all of the work she and others had done was in vain. It seemed that the fight for independence and equality was doomed to nothing but senseless violence. King's death was widely viewed as a catastrophic defeat for the Civil Rights Movement. Wherever Nina looked, great leaders and orators of the Black Movement were harassed, killed, falsely imprisoned, or monitored by the clandestine operations of the FBI, under J. Edgar Hoover.

The end of 1968 also saw Nina and Andrew Stroud's relationship strained beyond repair. She and Stroud were more business partners than they were lovers, and Nina no longer felt the same emotion for Stroud that she did in the beginning of their marriage. Her exhausting pace left little time for her to reflect on the matter or attempt any sort of reconciliation. Stroud, for his part, seemed more concerned with promoting his wife than loving her. He controlled all Nina's finances, including the businesses he had set up in her name, and ruled over her career like an emperor. Nina's increasing mood swings also caused him to be less than sympathetic toward her, and the two began to fight constantly. The fights, not just verbal, rapidly spiraled into physical violence. According to many witnesses in the company that traveled with the couple, Nina threw just as many punches and slaps as she received. The terrible situation between the couple endured for many months, despite a full concert schedule, tours in Europe, and further album releases by RCA.

RCA recorded the concert that Nina gave just a few days after the death of Dr. Martin Luther King. Playing at the Westbury Music Fair in New York, Nina dedicated the performance to King's memory. The album, 'Nuff Said, quickly became a smash success for Nina in Europe.

Her version of the song from the musical, Hair, earned her the second spot on the British music charts, and number one in the Netherlands. "Ain't Got No – I Got Life" is a medley of two songs and opened Nina's music to the younger audience who had enjoyed the musical from which it came. With that success, Nina felt the freedom to record something she had never done before: an album featuring her talent with the piano.

Nina Simone and Piano was released the same year, but was so radically different in style that it could not hope to duplicate the popularity of 'Nuff Said. Although it did not sell very well, it always held a special place in Nina's heart. Despite that, records continued to be released from RCA and Philips. To Love Somebody featured two Bee Gees songs covered by Nina, as well as the famous Pete Seeger song, "Turn! Turn! Turn!"

Nina gained another spot on the British music charts as she continued performing concerts across the United States. The pressure to perform and complete her music contracts, a point that she and Stroud argued about endlessly, finally erupted into a major fight with her husband. In September of 1970, Nina was more tired than she had ever been in her life. She begged Stroud for a break and a chance to rest. Focused on the timeline that her contracts spelled out, Andrew could see no way to grant Nina's request. They both left to attend the Newport Jazz Music Festival, in Rhode Island, but Nina was at her breaking point. The couple continued to argue all the way home and Stroud eventually left Nina alone in their home in New York. Nina removed her wedding band, left it on a table in the bedroom, and took a cab to the airport. She fled from both her husband and daughter, seeking much needed rest in the island country of Barbados.

[5]
The Musician Abroad

Nina's separation from Stroud in 1970 marked a major turning point in her life. She spent two weeks enjoying the beaches, water, and accommodations of the Caribbean before she returned home. Initially, she did not believe that her marriage was over. She hoped that her abrupt exit from the country would force Stroud to realize that she was serious when she said that she needed a vacation. She had left notice about her location with Cohen in New York and was surprised when Stroud never contacted her. As her vacation came to a close, she waited to hear from her husband. She had a concert to play in San Francisco and the date was well known. When Stroud did not call, she left Barbados and flew to New York to prepare for the upcoming show.

Her house seemed abandoned. She entered to find that the lights were off and Stroud's belongings were gone. He had left, taking their daughter. Nina had no idea where they had gone. She could not bear to stay in the house alone, so she secured an apartment in New York City until her flight to San Francisco the next day. The concert was tense and difficult for her as she tried to make sense of the mess her life had rapidly become.

Nina later found her daughter, Lisa, with relatives of Stroud. Though mother and daughter were reunited, Nina spoke with her husband only through their attorney. Stroud refused to speak with her personally. Nina also discovered that she would have to deal with other difficulties as well. She was in deep trouble with the IRS, who claimed that she had not paid taxes on large portions of her income. Her husband had access to all of her financial dealings and she had no idea how to begin addressing the accusations. Stroud's control of her money was so complete that she did not even have access to a bank account. Further complicating matters, Nina discovered that many of her tax records had been destroyed in a mysterious fire.

Nina was effectively impoverished. She only had what cash she made from her current shows. Unsure how she should proceed, she called her brother, Samuel, and fled to Philadelphia in the hope that her family could help. Samuel agreed to step in for Stroud as Nina's manager, though he had little experience in the job. Nina communicated with her lawyer, Cohen, by phone, but found that Andrew's grip on her finances was absolute. There was little that she could do to gain access to her business accounts. If she and her husband were to divorce, it was certain that she would lose a great deal of the wealth she had earned. As Nina began to deal with the painful truths that confronted her, she was at a complete loss for a solution. All she could do was continue to meet her concert obligations. She planned a European tour for 1971.

In a final blow to Nina's stability, she had a terrible argument with her father. She had always looked upon him with love, but when she heard that he claimed to be the only reason why the Waymon family survived financially, she became enraged. Nina's mother had worked very hard during the Depression to keep her family afloat. Nina had also steadfastly sent money to both of her parents throughout her performing career. Now that her husband had disappeared with most of that money, hearing her father take credit for her hard work was too much to accept. She left the house, vowing never to speak with her father again.

Nina finished her European tour and returned to Barbados whenever she could. It became a haven for her. The pace of her concert performances slowed somewhat and she was increasingly able to take time away to rest. Her financial situation had not improved, though, and she had to return to the time when she survived from the income provided by individual performances. Her record label continued to produce albums, but much of the money was diverted to accounts owned by her husband.

Nina and Stroud divorced in 1972. The marriage was over, but the fight for stability had just begun. That year proved to be tragic for Nina in many ways. Her father died in October, after a long battle against cancer. They had never had a chance to reconcile, despite repeated calls from her family. Nina was unable to forgive him and she kept her vow, never visiting him through his illness. Though on the surface her attitude seemed cold, Nina later dedicated a performance to her father and sang a song in his honor. A week later, Nina's sister Lucille died as well. Also suffering from cancer, Lucille had largely kept the illness a secret. Nina was numb with grief. Everything that she cared about seemed to be falling apart.

Nina finally decided that she could no longer stand to call the United States her permanent home. After surviving the disintegration of her marriage, her family, and the political movements that had meant so much to her, she now believed that her country engaged in a senseless war in Vietnam. It was further disintegration. She added her voice to the protest concerts opposing the violence, but it seemed to be a losing battle. In addition, the IRS threats of prosecution for tax evasion became increasingly dire. She took her daughter and fled again to Barbados, one of the few places that had ever brought her comfort.

During her return visit, she began a lengthy affair with the first Prime Minister of Barbados, Errol Barrow. Although he was married, Nina found comfort in his calm demeanor and lavish wealth. She desperately desired to have someone take care of her. The affair lasted for two years. During that time, Nina became increasingly erratic. She left her daughter with family friends of the Barrows, and Lisa saw little of her mother. Although Nina appeared for her concert dates, she was often late to appear on stage and her outbursts aimed at audiences became less tolerated by the critics. Her relationship with Barrow eventually disintegrated as well. Nina began to demand more of his affections and he could ill afford the scandal in his political career, should it become public. He eventually asked her to leave the house that he had provided for her and Lisa.

After the release of It is Finished, Nina's last album with RCA, her contract was not renewed by the record label. Though she had recorded numerous hit songs with them, many felt that Nina's reputation had become tarnished by her political associations and her odd behavior on stage. Despite the honors she still received by many African American leaders for her contribution to the Black Movement, she left the United States in 1974 at the invitation of Miriam Makeba. Makeba, one of the many civil rights activists Nina had befriended, offered Nina a way out.

Nina and her daughter were welcomed in Liberia with great fanfare. Within just a few days she met many of the heads of state, ministers, wealthy elite, and the President of the country. Nina believed that Liberia would become her permanent home. Without the pressure to perform musically, she began to look for a husband who could provide the lifestyle to which she had become accustomed. There were several suitors, but C. C. Dennis seemed the most promising. The son of a prominent Liberian official, Dennis was both wealthy and respected. He had every intention of marrying Nina, and declared so in a public and dramatic fashion. Nina soon learned, however, that he had strange notions of what constituted a proper wife. After an embarrassing intimate encounter with him, which culminated in a social scandal, she broke off the affair.

Liberia also introduced Nina to a branch of spirituality that she felt more closely aligned her to her African roots. On the advice of a friend, she traveled to see a traditional medicine man in the hopes of making amends with the spirit of her father. The shaman seemed to know very specific details about Nina's relationship with her father, which convinced her to trust his advice. The medicine man prescribed a three day ritual for Nina, one that would reacquaint her with her father's spirit and allow the process of forgiveness to begin. Nina followed it faithfully and later wrote that the spirit of John Waymon visited her. For the rest of her life, Nina always believed that her father visited and guided her during her darkest days. Those around Nina reported that she would occasionally speak aloud to her father. It became a behavior that many considered, at the very least, odd.

Nina left Liberia in 1976, moving to Switzerland with her daughter. She wanted Lisa to have a better education and felt that a boarding school would be best for that purpose. Nina and Lisa's relationship had always been rather tenuous, as Nina's lifestyle and concert obligations kept her away for long periods of time. Lisa, who would later go on to establish a career of her own on stage, always felt that her mother was a distant figure in her life. As Lisa entered boarding school, Nina continued to perform at concerts whenever she could. Her financial difficulties had not improved and the IRS in the United States continued to pursue its actions against her. She stayed away from her homeland, as much to evade her memories as she did to protect herself from legal action. Her mental state continued to move between high and low, often paralyzing her with terrible panic attacks. Her actions during her performances showed signs of the strain that she was under, though her music lost none of its beauty and flair.

The end of the 1970s was a difficult time for Nina. No longer attached to a record label, she performed at multiple venues for the funds necessary to keep her daughter in school and maintain her lifestyle. She traveled from Switzerland to Liberia and throughout Europe, always in search of work and love. She had several short affairs with men, most of which ended badly. In one incident, she was left beaten on a hotel room floor in London, by a lying suitor who only wanted to take advantage of her fame. She found herself in the hospital with reports that she had tried to commit suicide. She realized then that she had to take control of her life, without the benefit of a manager or a record label.

When she was hired by British jazz club, she began to tour exclusively through various cities in Europe. Most who witnessed those shows were completely unaware that Nina lived hand-to-mouth. Though her performances were exceptional, she was paid scant wages for them. Her behavior on stage, often at crowds who goaded such responses, continued to fuel the rumors that she was unstable. She was unsure how to proceed, so when her ex-husband called her to arrange a tour, she conceded. She trusted that his management skills could see her through the difficult times she experienced. She hoped for a triumphant return to her early success.

Nina arrived in the United States only to find that the IRS was ready to pursue its claims against her. Though Andrew promised that all would be well, Nina was forced to plead guilty to two tax evasion charges so that other charges would be dropped. She felt humiliated and only performed a few shows before she fled from the country again, returning to Switzerland. Over the next few years, Nina continued to perform sporadically, in Europe as well as in the United States. She moved to Paris in 1981.

Nina's life through the 1980s was defined by the struggle to climb back to the successes of her early career. She managed to release two albums, from different labels, that consisted of studio sessions as well as recorded music from her concerts. Using film footage, as well as interviews, she also began to release videos of her concerts. Most of these efforts met with mixed success, usually due to lack of financial backing by a major record label.

Nina's infamous reputation as a feisty diva followed her wherever she performed. She was often the subject of scorn and cruel ridicule in the media. Biographers close to Nina would later reveal that she suffered from a severe chemical imbalance. Finally diagnosed privately in the 1980s, she received medication for the imbalance. It helped to stabilize her moods, but it was far from a cure-all. She suffered bouts of depression as well as mania throughout the rest of her life.

In 1987, Nina Simone became a household name again, but not for the reasons she wished. In a promotional campaign, the fashion house Chanel used a song from her first album to promote its perfume in a commercial. A whole new generation was introduced to a song from early in Nina's career, "My Baby Just Cares for Me." Nina, however, had to fight to be paid the royalties that she was due from the record label who owned her song. Her original contract with Syd Nathan seemed ironclad. Fortunately, that contract did not include advertising rights. After a battle in court, Nina was paid a single sum for her song's use, but it was probably far less than the piece was worth. As the public clamored for the song, which played endlessly on the radio throughout Europe, it became a best-selling record in several countries.

Conclusion

Undaunted, Nina used the success from the ad campaign to launch her career anew. By the early 1990s, she released four new albums and could be seen in concert venues throughout the world. She had earned her place as a music legend and finally began to receive the recognition that she deserved, both as a musical genius and a steadfast fighter for Civil Rights. To chronicle this journey, she published her memoirs in 1992.

Although her health began to fail her, she toured widely in 1996. By that time, she had been embraced again as a symbol of African American power and pride. She had also been awarded the rights to over 50 of her own songs in a court decision in 1995. She was invited to attend the 80th birthday party of Nelson Mandela in South Africa in 1998, alongside other musical legends like Michael Jackson and Stevie Wonder. As an entirely new industry of music arose in the United States in the 1990s, musicians as diverse as Lauryn Hill, Sade, and Jeff Buckley cited Nina Simone's work as profoundly influential in their careers.

In 1998 Nina was awarded an honorary degree in Philadelphia for both music and the humanities. Granted the title, Doctor of Music and Humanities, it was an honor long overdue a woman who had been denied a formal education. The honors came in rapid succession, however, as Nina received the Diamond Award for Excellence in Music from the Association of African American Music, as well as being inducted into the Grammy Hall of Fame, both in the year 2000.

A performer to the end, Nina gave a series of concerts in 2001, though she was profoundly ill. She played in Paris, the United States, and in England. Her illness was evident by this point, but she toured the world with a diva's grace and style. She gave her last live performance in the summer of 2002.

In an ironic twist, the Curtis Institute granted Nina an honorary diploma in 2003. By then, Nina was bedridden with the cancer that claimed her life. Nina's daughter accepted the honor for her mother. Nina spent her final days in her home, in southern France. She died on April 21st in 2003. Nina's legacy as a steadfast performer and champion of Civil Rights lives on in the music she left behind, often featured in film soundtracks and as remixes. It can also be felt in the numerous lives she touched in the music industry, both in the United States and throughout the world.

Bibliography

Brun-Lambert, David. Nina Simone: The Biography. Aurum Press, 2009.

Cohodas, Nadine. Princess Noire: The Tumultuous Reign of Nina Simone. Pantheon Books, 2010.

Eliott, Richard. Icons of Pop Music: Nina Simone. Equinox Publishing Ltd., 2003.

Hampton, Sylvia and Nathan, David. Nina Simone: Break Down & Let It All

Hang Out. Sanctuary Publishing Limited, 2004.

MTV

Nina Simone Database. Copyright 2014, Mauro Boscarol.

http://www.boscarol.com/ninasimone/pages/php/alb_orig.php

Nina Simone Discography. Copyright 2014, Allmusic.

http://www.allmusic.com/artist/nina-simone-mn0000411761/discography

Nina Simone Discography. Copyright 2014, Viacom International Inc.

http://www.mtv.com/artists/nina-simone/discography/

Simone, Nina and Cleary, Stephen. I Put a Spell on You: The Autobiography of Nina Simone. Da Capo Press, 1991.

Made in United States
Orlando, FL
27 January 2022